NIRVANA

PHOTOGRAPHS BY **STEVE GULLICK** AND **STEPHEN SWEET**

www.visiononpublishing.com

PEOPLE SAY PHOTOGRAPHS DON'T LIE.
THAT'S BOLLOCKS.

It's rare that I recognise anyone from photos. The way someone glances at you, the smear of their eye shadow, the flop of a hairstyle... these are the last things I notice about a person, the last points of interest for me. What matters is the way someone invades your body space, the lilt in their voice as they discuss the new Pixies compilation, the nervous laugh. I'm a music critic. I listen to people's voices.

I find it almost impossible to recognise people by their looks, even people I've spent countless hours with and imbibed wrongful accusations for. The way someone flutters their eyelids, the way fists are clenched and unlocked, the shadow a guitar makes as it's being raised up high to be smashed through the floor... I never notice these aspects of life. If I did, maybe I'd be Stephen.

Here's my take on history books. I hate them. I fucking hate them.

I hate anything that means something has ceased to exist. I don't want to let go. I don't like the idea that a moment in time can be captured, stilled – in other words, become a moment in time. What was Nirvana? A celebration of much that was glorious about our lives. How can that be captured in a couple of grainy frames? It can't. I know. Any photograph's resonance rests with the receiver, although sometimes it can help bring into sharper relief otherwise smudgy memories or ideas. I

love the photos in this book because Steve and Stephen were part of my growing and living through the late 80s and 90s. I hate them because I never thought I'd find myself in a museum until I was old enough to wave my Zimmer frame around. Live and learn.

'Come on over and do the twist / Overdo it and have a fit / Love you so much it makes me sick / Come on over and shoot the shit' – Aneurysm

Those two words: Olympia and Nirvana. They go well together, don't they?

Musicians, when asked about what certain songs mean to them, sometimes answer truthfully and recall the studio that the recording took place in, the Chinese take-away they'd eaten beforehand, the number of takes it took to get a particular snare sound. I can sympathise but I also like my glamour. I don't want the mundane. Make up a story! Entertain! You're in the damn entertainment industry, after all. Life is about perception. Your reality is what counts.

Sure, I can tell you stories about the photographs in this book.

November 1993. I'm lost in Massachusetts. I arrive at a tiny, almost unlit airport in the middle of nowhere. A random car announces itself as a cab and takes me deep into the woods. Imagine my relief

when I see the bright lights of a hockey stadium shining through the gloom. I walk up to the door and announce myself. I am Everett True! Backstage it's as awkward and intimate as ever, a few musicians sitting around, the usual welcoming faces among the crew. Was Steve Gullick there? I have no idea. The photos indicate he was. It was odd we were there at all. We weren't covering the story for Melody Maker. We weren't covering the story for anyone. Kurt had pleaded with me to 'come as a friend, not as a journalist', if I wanted to travel with Nirvana again. So I asked Steve to take appropriate shots – photos that he enjoyed, nothing fancy, just his usual genius. He was with Mercury Rev singer David Baker, a fact that later displeased Kurt. I was with Sebadoh singer Lou Barlow, a fact that later pleased Kurt.

Bethlehem and Springfield were two of the venues where Kurt inveigled my presence on stage – yelling down the microphone, trying to cope with Kurt's left-handed guitar placed on my shoulders upside down, mindful of the warning from tour manager Alex McLeod that I was 'fucking dead' if I smashed it like last time. The kids looked on bemused, and Pat Smear lapped up my faux-punk actions like the proverbial Cheshire. Springfield is where my favourite sequence of Nirvana photos were taken. Steve worked like a god, relaxed for once, while I tried to look cool and failed miserably. Later, a whole bunch of us celebrated our kinship by holding a Queen

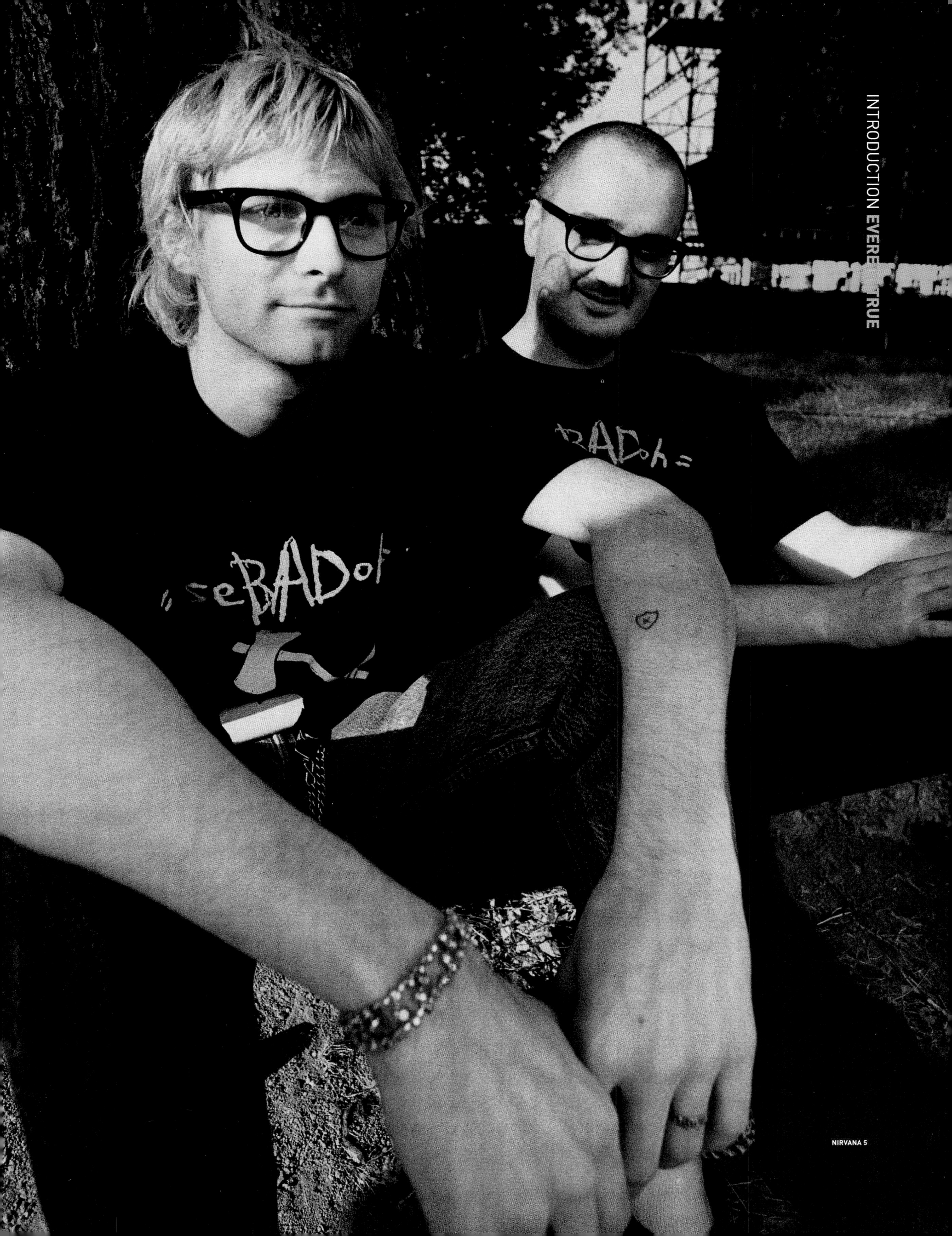

> " THIS IS A BOOK OF
> IMAGES OF NIRVANA,
> TAKEN BY TWO MEN WITH
> SOUL AND APTITUDE.
> YES, THAT'S A
> RECOMMENDATION."

party on the tour bus, where Krist presented Steve with a fragment of a TV screen for doing the best Freddie Mercury impression. These shows were super-fine. The Breeders and Half Japanese supported, Lori played a sweet cello and someone blew smoke rings. Everyone was on much better terms than has been reported since, even if Kurt did travel in a different van from Krist and Dave. When we arrived in New York a few days later – Steve had flown off, doubtless to break a few more hearts – Kurt offered me his hotel floor to sleep on, and insisted on me singing at that night's show, even though my voice had completely disappeared. My performance was later described as 'truly terrible'. Alex, incidentally, was the best fucking tour manager a band could ever want.

I travelled often with Steve and Stephen. Between the three of us we probably documented the career of Nirvana more than any other team of music reporters. Like that matters. We would catch planes across America, run rampant through whatever bar was passing and with whichever musicians deigned to let us

amuse them, and somehow managed to record what was happening. People remembered what we did afterwards. Why? I have no idea, but perhaps it helped that we didn't hide our individuality. It seems the music business is constantly engaged in one long struggle to hide its protagonists' individuality. Everything becomes rounded off, all sharp angles and corners removed so they don't unsettle, especially at the level where Nirvana eventually found themselves. There's no room for humanity, and any soul is discouraged. Maybe that's why the three of us got along so well with Kurt, Krist and Dave and some of those around. We didn't like to pretend we were people we weren't.

There are photos in this book that capture the essence of Nirvana better than I could ever hope to in my writing, but I'm damned if I'm going to say which ones. Unguarded moments, that's what most people go for. Kurt plays on his guitar backstage in Springfield. Someone lights someone else's cigarette. The three musicians horse around on a bed at the Dalmacia. Krist looks concerned. A whole group of

friends mug it up for the camera. I couldn't give a crap.

December 1989. The whole year was spent in a frenzy of expectation and desire. I couldn't believe that so many cool long-haired American rockers wanted to party with me. On the night of the third, there were several of us standing at the side of the London Astoria stage, waiting to leap into the crowd during a dull spot in Nirvana's set. We had some wait coming. Nirvana might have been the opening band at Sub Pop's Lamefest UK showcase, but that hardly mattered. No fanfare, no spotlight, no dry ice, just a sound that tore our hearts apart. Kurt was, as Mr Sweet wrote, 'in turn full of terror and gentleness, [and] threw himself around like nothing existed outside of each moment he played and sang.' Bored of waiting, our backstage troupe decided to jump off stage anyway – Sub Pop PR Anton Brookes, Sounds journalist Keith Cameron, Matt Lukin from Mudhoney, mighty man mountain Tad Doyle and me. The crowd parted as one when they saw Tad lumbering towards them, and the singer landed straight on top

of the luckless bassist, who then had to be scraped from the floor. Mudhoney were peerless that night, at the peak of their raw power. Tad was as ferociously entertaining as ever. Yet there was something so unsettling and contrary about Nirvana, you couldn't help but pay attention.

October 1990. Every emerging US rock band stayed at the Dalmacia, particularly those looked after by Anton. Situated in Shepherd's Bush, it was infamous for locking the door on groups that returned home too late. The Four Seasons it was not. By the time Stephen took these shots, Nirvana were already well-established on the UK live circuit. Kurt acted the pissy rock star towards Stephen, refusing to cooperate with someone he saw as part of the music industry machine. The situation was only rescued by Krist's usual good humour, messing with the bedspread... and the fact Stephen was not as Kurt had portrayed him. The Nottingham Polytechnic show was rare good fun. Stephen and I were exceedingly drunk. Kurt pulled me up on stage to encore with the band on vocals and guitar while he and Krist banged the

drums. The crowd looked confused, but thoroughly got into the spirit of the party when the two Nirvana musicians ended up with a spot of instrument smashing. Afterwards, Nirvana convinced their support L7 that Stephen and I were not journalists there to interview them, but mere friends and wasters. Boy, were they mad when they found out the truth.

Let's go back to the beginning. Anton Brookes of Bad Moon PR sent me a handful of Sub Pop singles at the end of '88. I liked them, found myself dancing like a Birthday Party fan on the table in the reviews room of Melody Maker to them, especially the holy three of Mudhoney, Nirvana and the U-Men. Anton wanted a couple of journalists to fly out to Seattle in February 1989 to cover the burgeoning Seattle scene. He wanted the Stud Brothers, iconoclastic colleagues of mine (and far better writers, back then). There were two of them, too expensive. So I picked myself instead.

Around that time, I became reviews editor at MM. Art editor Brett Lewis instructed me to bring on some new photographers. He

Notting Hill, September 1991
Photo by Steve Gullick

was bigger and feistier than me (threw a mean punch too if you nicked his drugs), so I obeyed him. One of those smudges was a former drama student and window cleaner called Stephen Sweet. It so happened I was dating a girl studying art in Newcastle, and Geordie Stephen sometimes missed his old friends and family. He indulged my fantasies of being a rock star by not blowing the whistle on my antics, so we ended up taking a lot of trips up North together.

September 1992. Stephen and I have to take a two-hour cab ride across LA to some dusty warehouse full of mouldy devil and angel costumes because we're thinking Kurt and Courtney together would make a perfect Christmas cover for Melody Maker. Our mistake. The pair agree to a joint interview simply because it's me and I introduced them to one another, but pose together? No. Stephen is too much the gent to insist or to be sneaky, but Kurt paints Diet Grrrl on Frances Bean's stomach and he and Courtney pose separately with their child, so the bailiffs are kept from his door for a few months longer. The session and interview take place at the couple's Hollywood house, situated halfway up a hill with an elevator. My friend Eric from Courtney's band is there, amusing Frances. A Mavis Staples album sits at the front of Kurt's record collection. He's half asleep when we arrive, but Courtney is as lively and bitchy as ever. For the interview I share the bed with the duo, opening fan mail and watching Ren & Stimpy on the television.

That was in the evening. I don't recall what happened to Stephen. Maybe the photo shoot took place on a different afternoon. Wicker chairs were involved, possibly. Anyway, we got the exclusive and it felt very sweet, I can tell you.

I started using Steve Gullick for Melody Maker in 1991. It was because Stephen and I felt guilty for drinking the mini-bar in his Valencia hotel room dry when we first encountered one another. The same trip, all of us danced on stage in front of five thousand Spanish kids, high on alcohol and delirium - and Steve was probably one of the few in our party that weekend that didn't throw a punch at me. (Unlike Stephen.) You have to admire that. When we next met, it was on Blackfriars Bridge near King's Reach Tower and Steve had just heard his paper, Sounds, had closed. I liked him and I liked Sounds. So I asked him to join MM. How couldn't you? Steve shook with an intensity that few people in their right minds could ever want to attain. He was unshaven, young, and old-fashioned at his core (i.e. decent). I was shaking too. It was 10am and I hadn't had a drink yet.

August and September 1991. The previous year had been awesome, but '91 was even better. Nirvana had reached the pinnacle of their personal success, large enough to attract attention but not too large to play small venues. We smashed up hotel rooms together. I threw up in their tour van. I got carried over Krist's shoulders for miles in

LA with a plastic bag hooked onto my ears to catch the vomit. Nevermind was recorded, and even though the production on it now sounds like a less offensive Mötley Crüe, it certainly delighted us at the time. The Reading festival performance was excellent and fun too. It wasn't 1992 yet (meaning Nirvana's management hadn't banned every last person who could possibly like the band from their proximity - except me, of course) and Steve was allowed access to the stage while Kurt created his usual mayhem. He leapt into drum kits, sang with Eugene from the Vaselines and wandered through the backstage area with his arm in a sling.

I bumped into Steve, and Nirvana, again in NYC. Steve was out there covering the Candyskins for MM with a future editor of Select, and I was chancing my arm as usual – flown out to America under false pretences because I said I'd deliver a Nirvana interview to my editors who had finally begun to understand how big the Aberdeen (NOT Seattle) trio were going to be. I was there to interview the Breeders. I didn't even know which coast of America Nirvana were on at the time. It so happened Nirvana were playing at New York's Marquee Club the night after I arrived, something Steve and his colleague delighted in informing me at 4am that morning. All of Kurt's guitars broke and maybe Krist's bass as well, and for the encore, Mr Cobain ended up singing along to Dave's drums by himself. As Mr Gullick

" I LOVE THE PHOTOS IN THIS BOOK BECAUSE STEVE AND STEPHEN WERE PART OF MY GROWING AND LIVING THROUGH THE LATE EIGHTIES AND NINETIES. I HATE THEM BECAUSE I NEVER THOUGHT I'D FIND MYSELF IN A MUSEUM UNTIL I WAS OLD ENOUGH TO WAVE MY ZIMMER FRAME AROUND. LIVE AND LEARN."

memorably remarked at the time, it still sounded like a fucking choir. I introduced Kurt to Kim Deal, as he was a major fan of the Breeders' Pod album. He invited me along to travel with the band, and sing and dance and drink and chat and do all those purple-spangled things in between. It was a good time.

I don't like most photographs. I don't understand their purpose. They confuse and bemuse me, and not in a positive way. All my writing ever hoped to attain was a blurred snapshot of an event that in all probability never happened, certainly not in the way my mind recalls it. Photographs don't even have the grace to be like that. They're too in focus for my liking. Like it matters. I like the two Steves' pictures because, unusually, I think that no one else could have taken them. Are you telling me Kurt would have interacted with some fucking hack or soulless chameleon the same way? Fuck off. Doubtless he trusted Stephen and Steve because they were with me, but that certainly wasn't the only secret behind these photographs. Steve and Stephen have soul, and that soul is apparent on every page you flick through here, disinterested in your modern comfort.

June 1992. I'd shaved my head, the result of a drunken basketball bet with Urge Overkill in Chicago the week before. Courtney was along for the Scandinavian tour, something that didn't please Krist or Dave too much. The three of us – Kurtney

and me – walked along the perimeter of the outdoor stadium's fence, confiscating bootlegs and creating mischief. Afterwards, I found myself the only person allowed into the couple's hotel room. The interview between the three Nirvana members was strained. It was almost as if it was the first time the three had communicated for months. Kurt didn't want Steve to shoot him with his newly cropped hair, because he didn't want to be recognised at Nirvana's Reading Festival headline slot coming up in a few weeks time. The pair reached a compromise, which included Steve drawing in long hair on Kurt on the live photograph that was used in Melody Maker to accompany one of the best damn reviews I ever wrote.

I remember listening to the sound of support Teenage Fanclub warming up with a Big Star cover on the open-air stage outside, and contrasting it with the Nirvana soundcheck, a crew member taking Kurt's vocals as he hadn't shown. Or is that standard behaviour for big bands? Gullick and I took the remainder of the crew and band, minus Kurtney, up to a hillock where we messed around and laughed. All we suggested was that we 'could go out and play'. Afterwards, the whole entourage, including Teenage Fanclub and led by guitar tech Big John (formerly of the Exploited), enjoyed a karaoke session until very late indeed. The following day, I saw a 'grunge' covers band in a local bar do faithful interpretations of all the popular classics –

Everett, Kurt and Frances Bean,
Seattle, December 1993
Photo by Steve Gullick

Soundgarden, Stone Temple Plagiarists, Pearl Jam – all but Nirvana. The latter they covered in high-pitched, 'girlie' voices. The inference was obvious. Nirvana were fags.

I travelled often with Stephen and Steve to cover Nirvana. If I type that phrase often enough maybe it will attain a certain rhythm and style and then we can all finally move on.

July 1993. New York again, and Stephen and I were living it up at another New Music Seminar. I don't recall if this was the one where I gatecrashed a panel with a pair of flashing shades and shaven head, drank my way through an entire bottle of vodka supplied by the girls from Ben Is Dead fanzine, and hurled abuse at everyone standing for a straight hour. Maybe. Melody Maker had finally sent the Stud Brothers to finish the job they were promised so long ago, and Stephen was taking the photos. In one of the shots, Kurt is reading my Neil Young/Pearl Jam MM concert review that later caused arch-enemy Eddie Vedder to storm out of a Q interview. I sat in the lobby of Nirvana's NYC hotel and waited for Kurt to be done with all this bothersome press business so we could hang out. Other, much more established journalists were making a point of speaking to me (something they certainly don't bother with any more). Unbeknownst to me, Kurt was mistreating my friends, again counting down the minutes Stephen was allowed with the band, but fuck those rock star tosspots. We knew who we were and what soul we had, and we never stooped to making something as crap as MTV Unplugged either. Stephen got some great shots under duress in the 'horrible discipline' of a music industry hour, on the corner of West 42nd before it turned all Disney. Not that you need me to tell you that.

No, I didn't want any of this. All I ever wanted to do in my writing was to capture the enthusiasm I felt for music, the enthusiasm that moved my feet to take on strange directions while watching bands. Maybe that's Steve and Stephen's motivating factor. I strongly suspect so. Otherwise, why would I have bothered to travel with the pair so frequently? We played Tetris on plane rides, Tetris and cribbage – and neither of the photographers could out-drink me when it came to spirits. If they did, that gave me cause for concern. We looked after our own kind, and that included Nirvana. The feeling was mutual, I'm sure of it. I came from Olympia and so did Kurt and Krist, and that's why we understood one another. That's why these photos work where so many others don't. Or maybe it's just down to my own individual perception – I was there, remember? Maybe all of this is crap. I have no way of telling.

December 1993. A deeply unhappy Kurt tells me he had to throw the Tad band off Nirvana's US tour because of a spat between Tad's lady love and his own. 'What would you do?' he keeps asking. Steve and I are in town with Anton again, trying to organise a joint MM Christmas cover between Kurt and Eddie, kiss and make up. Pearl Jam cowardly pull out from playing the MTV special at Pier 48 at the last minute, so we're left hanging around for hours. We smoke boo with Cypress Hill and stifle yawns in the direction of pompous MTV middle-management people. In the end, we settle for a joint Kurt and Kim Deal interview. Steve is given precisely twelve frames to get the cover shot, but this time the fault lies with a stoned Kim, not Kurt. The live show is fine. I never liked the angel from the cover of In Utero, thought it pretentious, but didn't want to burst anyone's bubble. Eric from Hole, nanny Cali DeWitt and I conspire to have me run on stage during the band's set wearing an Eddie Vedder mask, but the management soon put a stop to such shenanigans. It's the last time either Steve or I would see Kurt alive, although the singer did phone me up at home a few days later on Christmas Day, mindful of an anti-Christmas rant I'd given him and Kim. 'You're the only one of our friends we could think of who'd be in,' he roared, laughing. 'How are you? Still miserable? Merry fucking Christmas!'

This is a book of images of Nirvana, taken by two men with soul and aptitude. Yes, that's a recommendation.

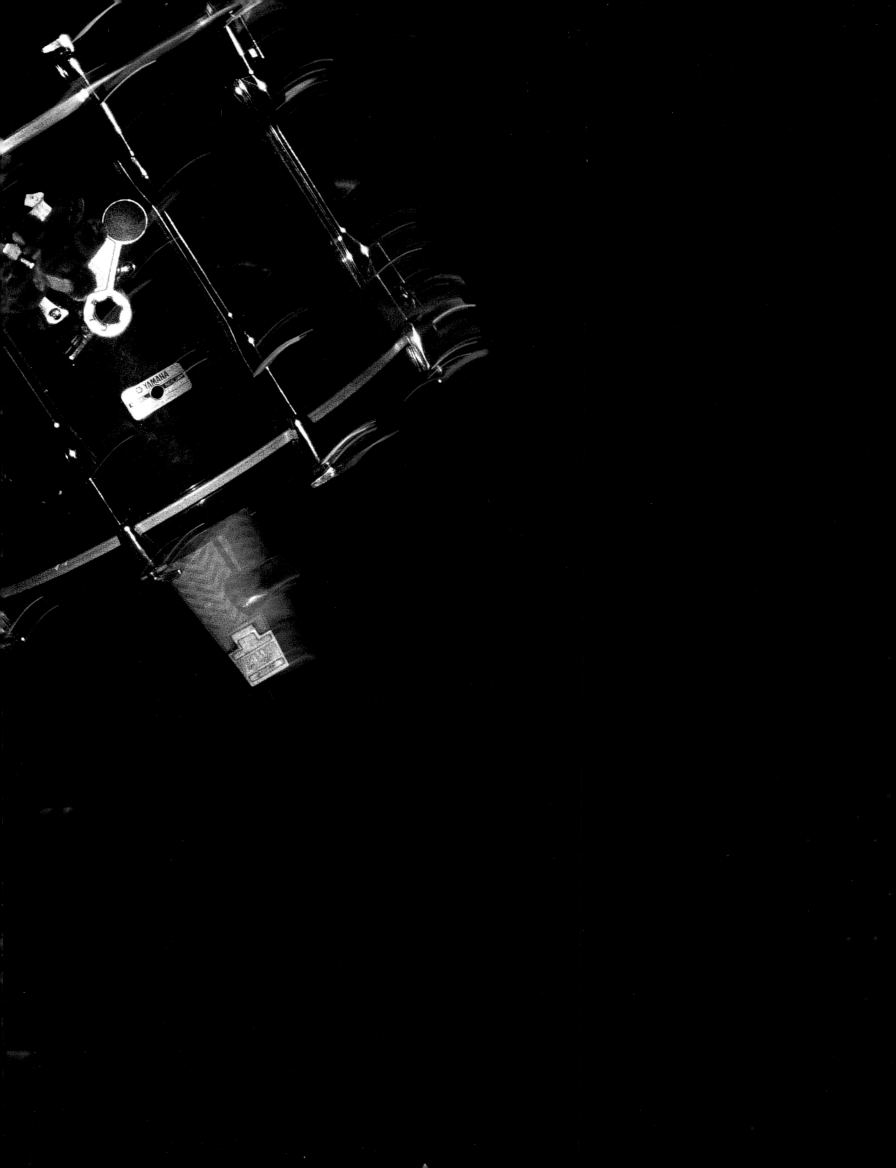

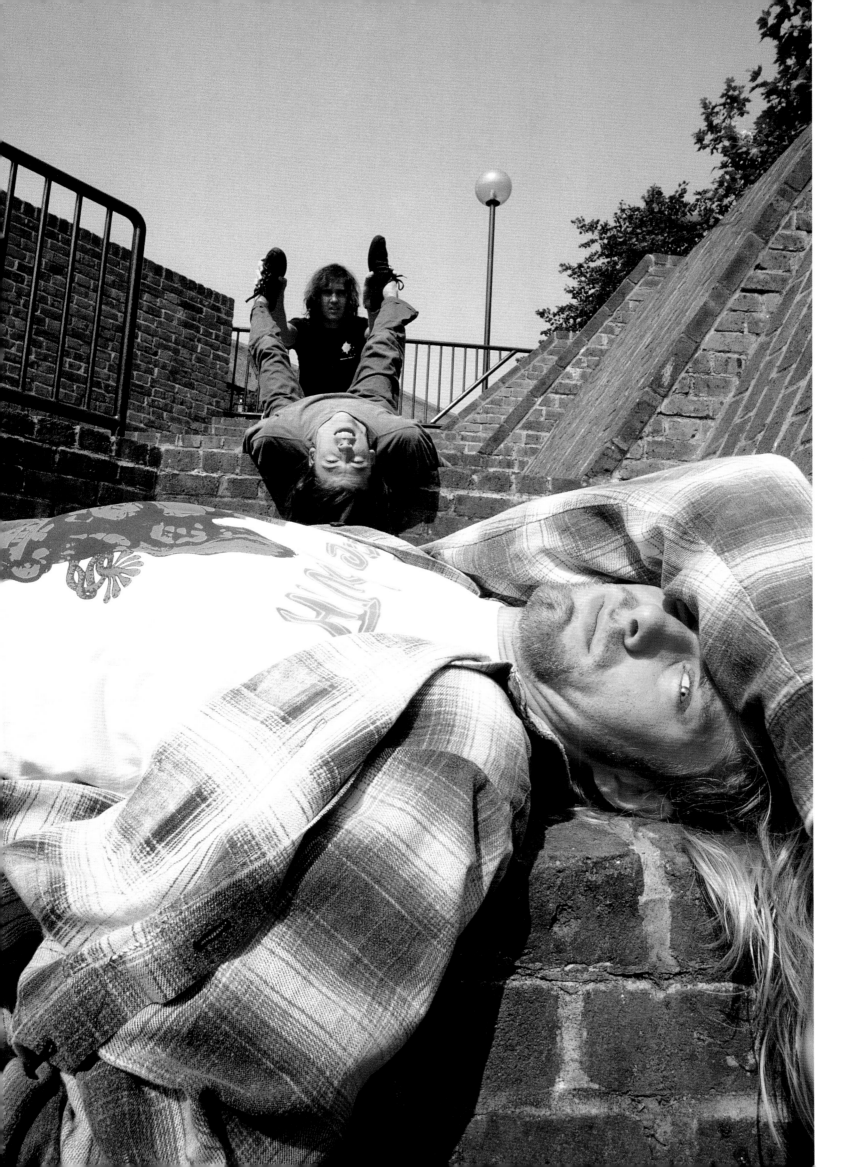

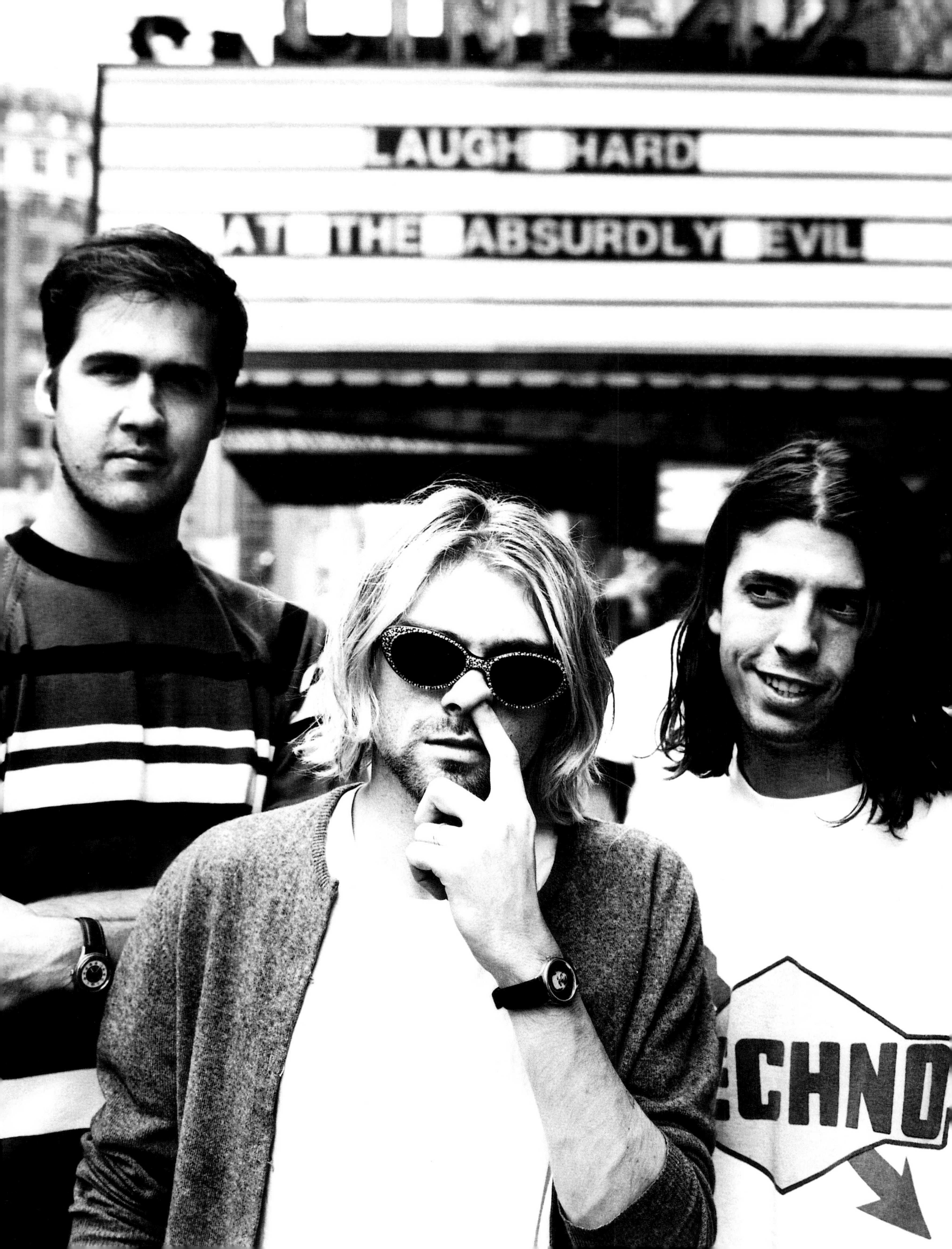
LAUGH HARD
AT THE ABSURDLY EVIL

T
YOU
RE

SAVOR KINDN
BECAUSE CRU
S ALWAYS P
LATER

TOYOTA

NYC POLICE

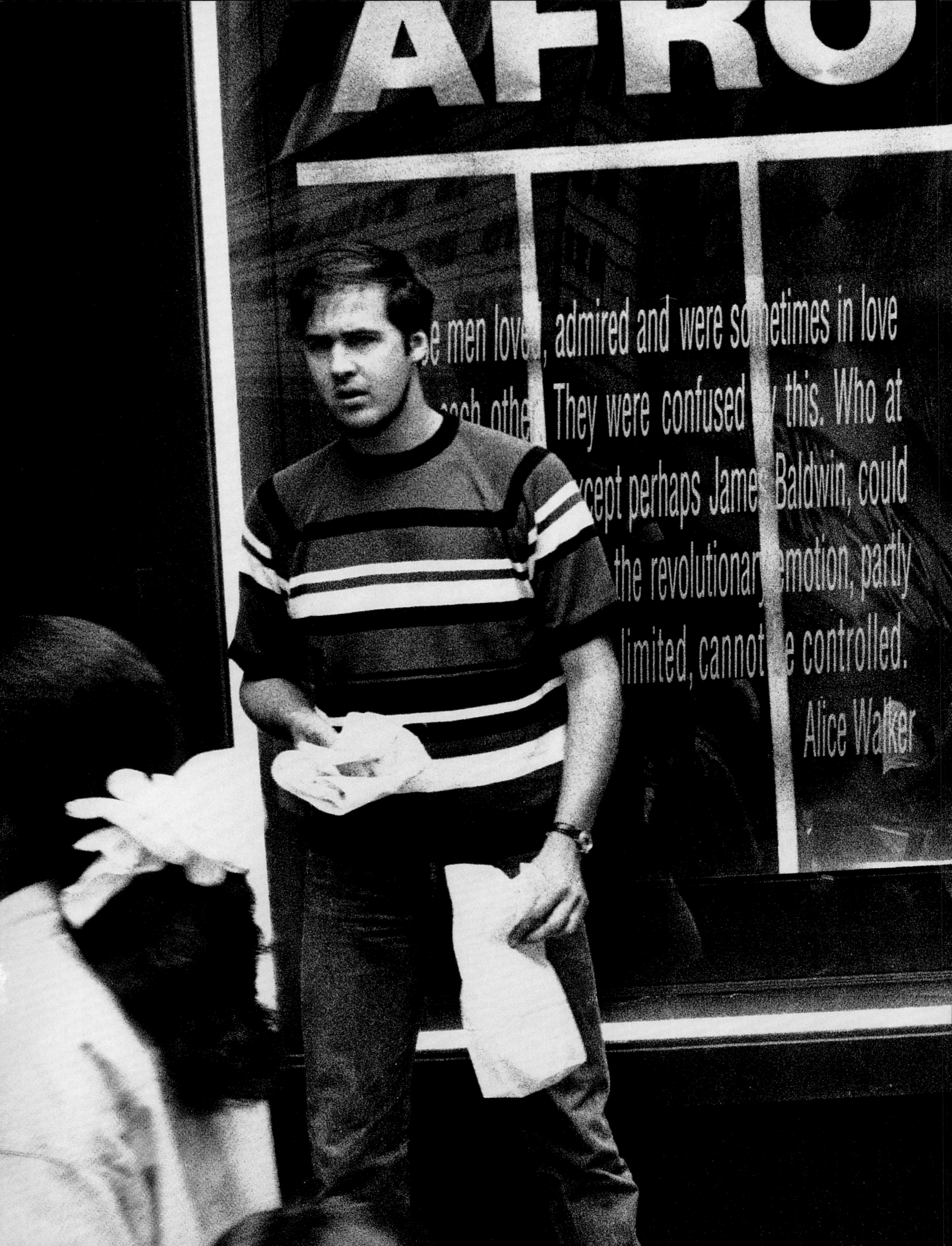

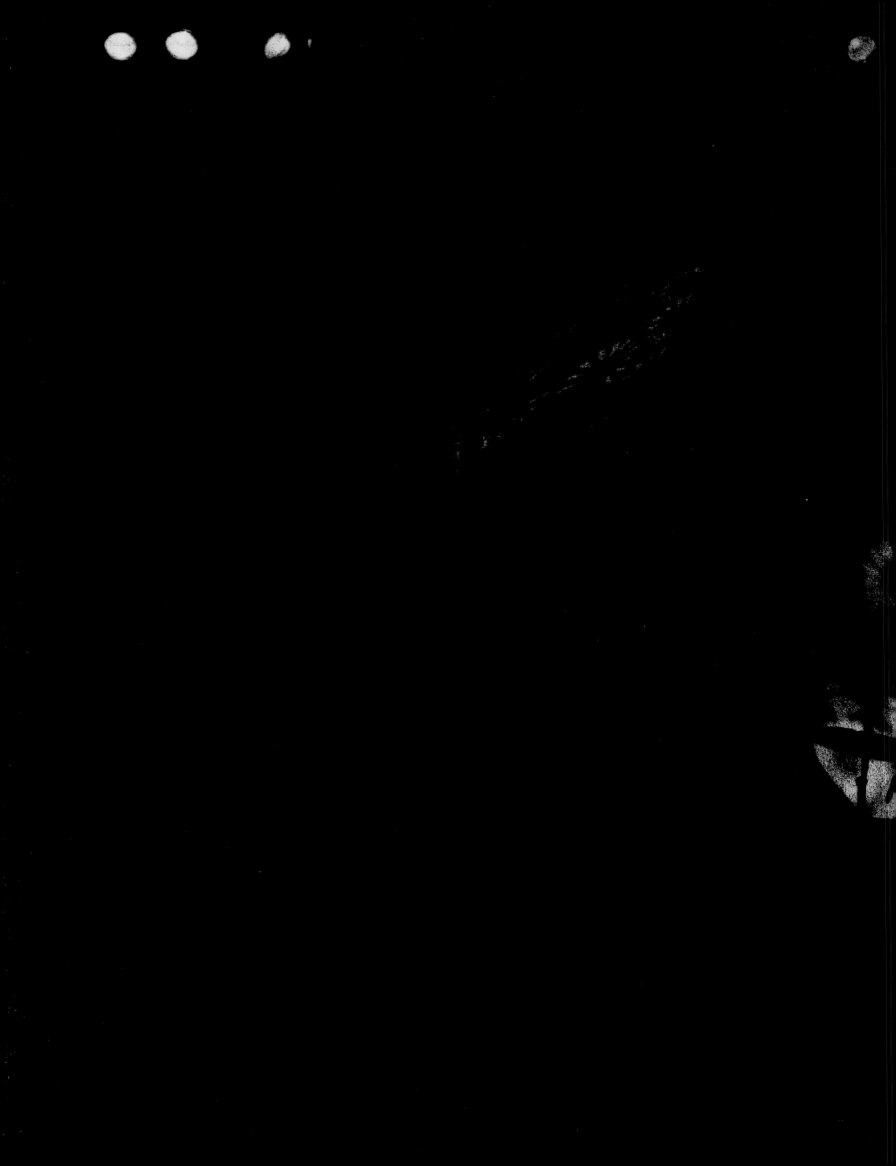

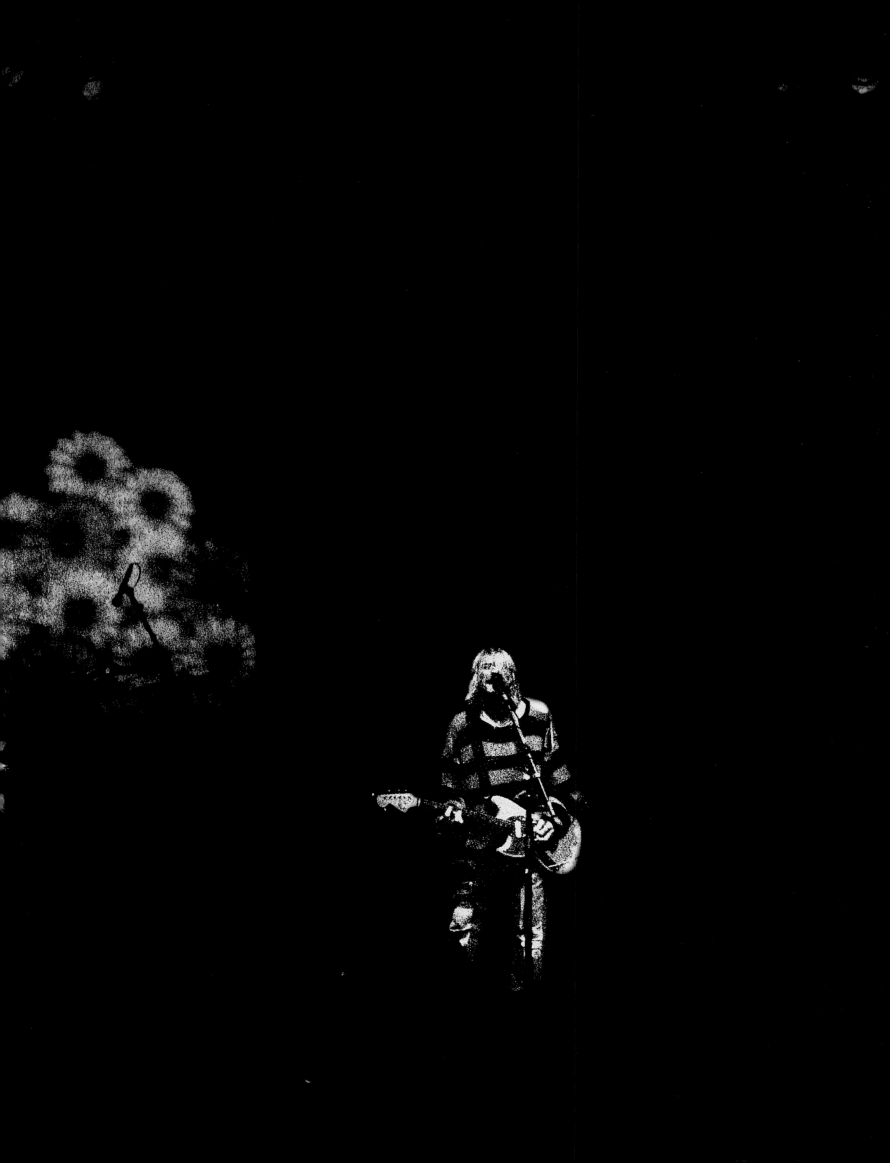

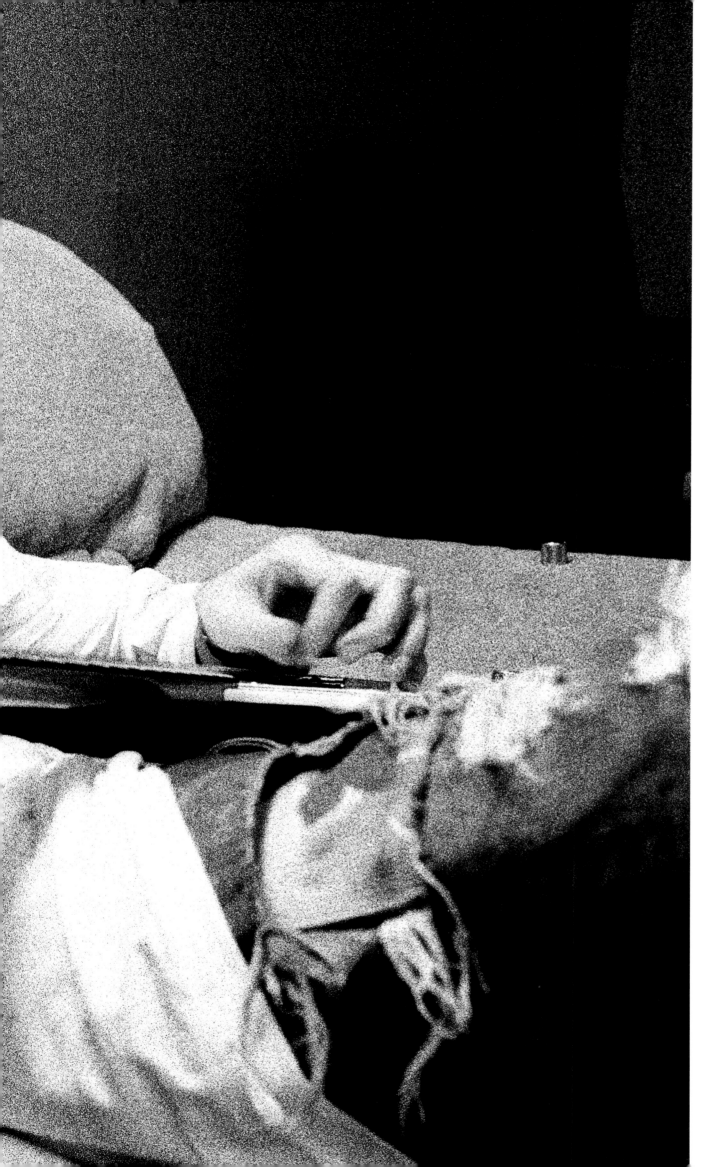

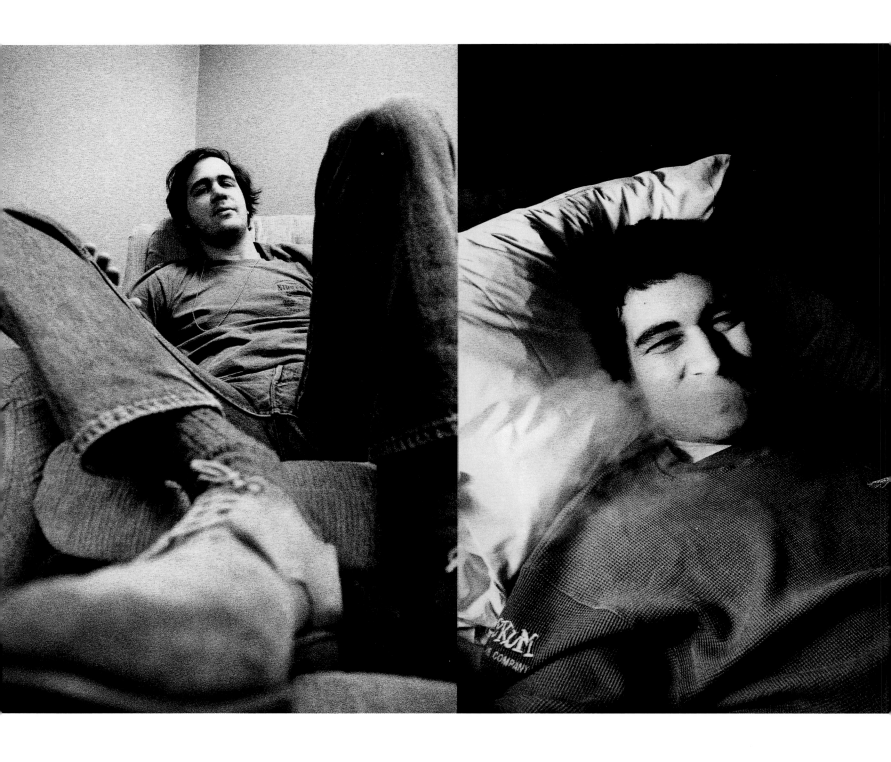

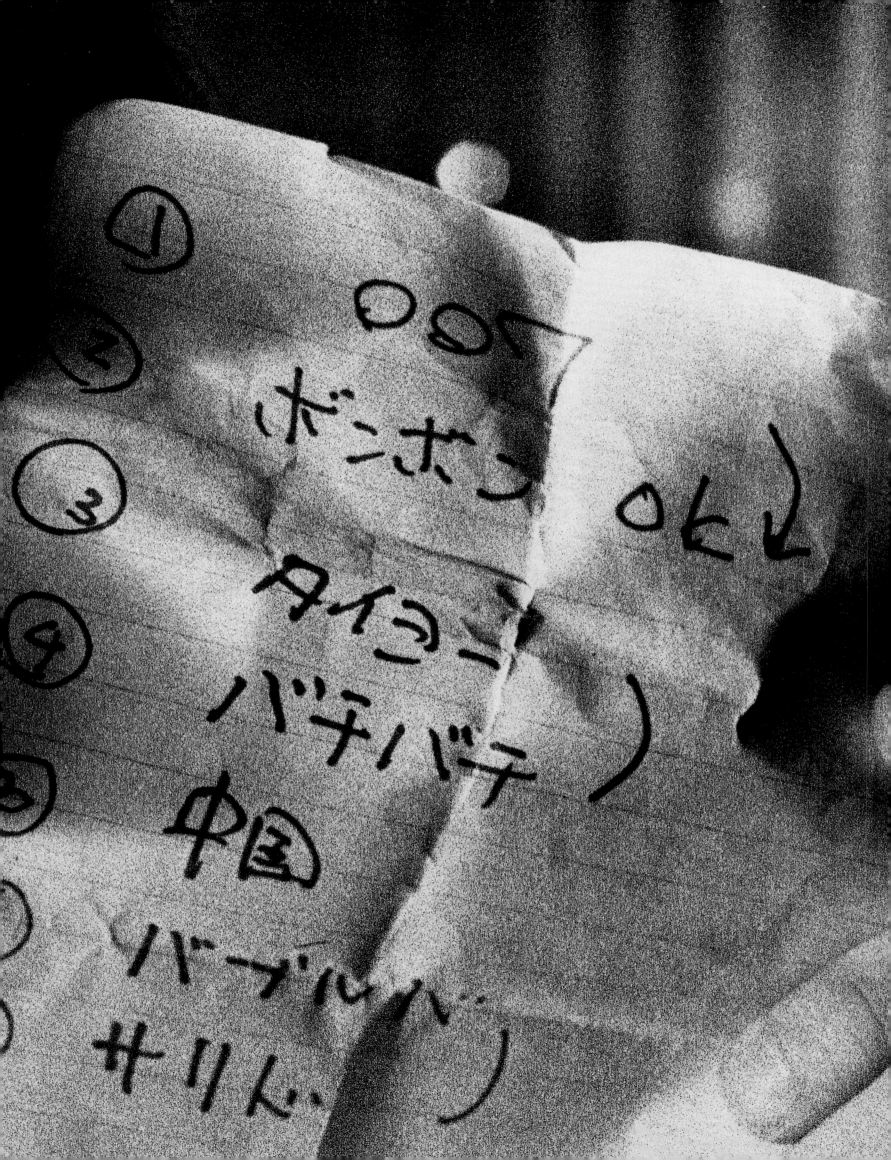

THANKS TO NIRVANA, EVERETT TRUE, ANTON BROOKES AND THE ONCE GREAT MELODY MAKER.

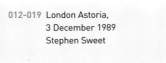

048-049   London Kilburn National,
          5 December 1991
          Steve Gullick

050-055   Notting Hill,
          4 September 1991
          Steve Gullick

056-071   Stockholm, June 1992
          Steve Gullick

072-077   Oslo, June 1992
          Steve Gullick

078-083   Stockholm, June 1992
          Steve Gullick

84-91   Hollywood, California,
          September 1992
          Stephen Sweet

092-109 New York City, 24 July 1993
Stephen Sweet

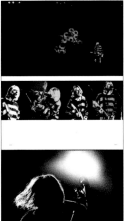

110-115 Roseland Ballroom,
New York City, 25 July 1993
Stephen Sweet

116-139 Springfield, Massachusetts
and Bethlehem, Pennsylvania,
9-10 November 1993
Steve Gullick

140-141   Bethlehem, Pennsylvania,
          9 November 1993
          Steve Gullick

142-153   MTV Pier 48 Show, Seattle,
          Washington,
          13 December 1993
          Steve Gullick

Cover   Springfield, Massachusetts,
            10 November 1993
            Steve Gullick
Back cover New York City, 24 July 1993
            Stephen Sweet

Photography
Steve Gullick and Stephen Sweet

Introduction
Everett True

Book Design
Martin@Fruit Machine

Creative Director
Kirk Teasdale

Project Manager
Sarah Marusek

Production
Steve Savigear and Emily Moore

Reprographics
AJD Colour Ltd

Print
The National Press, Jordan

Vision On would like to thank Briar, Diana, Lisa, Ed and Ronny; Alan, Nina and Suzanne at Proud Galleries; Andy, Nick and all the boys at AJD and Omar, Zaid, Zeina and Hani at the National Press, Jordan.

Nirvana first published in Great Britain in 2001 by Vision On Publishing Ltd
112-116 Old Street
London EC1V 9BG
T +44 20 7336 0766
F +44 20 7336 0966
www.visiononpublishing.com
info@visiononpublishing.com
www.gullickphoto.com

A CIP catalogue record for this book is avalible from the British Library.

ISBN 1 903399 17 3

www.visiononpublishing.com